SCHOLASTIC

studySMART™

Reading Skills Builder

Level K1
English

**Kama Einhorn &
Rozanne Lanczak Williams**

Text copyright © 2005 by Rozanne Lanczak Williams
Text copyright © 2011 by Kama Einhorn
Text copyright © 2012 by Scholastic Education International (Singapore) Private Limited. A division of Scholastic Inc.
Illustrations copyright © 2005, 2011 by Scholastic Inc.

Previously published as Success with Grammar series by Scholastic Inc.

All rights reserved. No part of this publication may be reproduced in whole or in part, or stored in a retrieval system, or transmitted in any form or by any means, electronic, mechanical, photocopying, recording, or otherwise without the written permission of the publisher.

For information regarding permission, write to:
Scholastic Education International (Singapore) Pte Ltd
81 Ubi Avenue 4, #02-28 UB.ONE, Singapore 408830
Email: education@scholastic.com.sg

For sales enquiries write to:

Latin America, Caribbean, Europe (except UK), Middle East and Africa
Scholastic International
557 Broadway, New York, NY 10012, USA
Email: intlschool@scholastic.com

Philippines
Scholastic Philippines
Penthouse 1, Prestige Tower, F. Ortigas Jr. Road, Ortigas Center, Pasig City 1605
Email: educteam@scholastic.com.ph

Asia (excluding India and Philippines)
Scholastic Asia
Plaza First Nationwide, 161, Jalan Tun H S Lee, 50000 Kuala Lumpur, Wilayah Persekutuan Kuala Lumpur, Malaysia
Email: international@scholastic.com

Rest of the World
Scholastic Education International (Singapore) Pte Ltd
81 Ubi Avenue 4 #02-28 UB.ONE Singapore 408830
Email: education@scholastic.com.sg

Visit our website: www.scholastic.com.sg

Australia
Scholastic Australia Pty Ltd
PO Box 579, Gosford, NSW 2250
Email: scholastic_education@scholastic.com.au

New Zealand
Scholastic New Zealand Ltd
Private Bag 94407, Botany, Auckland 2163
Email: orders@scholastic.co.nz

India
Scholastic India Pvt. Ltd.
A-27, Ground Floor, Bharti Sigma Centre,
Infocity-1, Sector 34, Gurgaon (Haryana) 122001, India
Email: education@scholastic.co.in

First edition: 2012
Reprinted: 2012, 2016

ISBN 978-981-07-1377-5

Welcome to SCHOLASTIC studySMART!

Reading Skills Builder gives your child a headstart in learning to read by equipping him with the skills needed to decode words easily and read fluently.

Phonics, word families and sight words are three essential skills that aid reading fluency. The understanding of phonics sound patterns leads to knowledge of word families. Knowledge of word families enhances your child's ability to recognize words. Quick recognition of sight words leads to faster decoding, which in turn leads to increased fluency and better comprehension.

This book introduces, teaches and reinforces common phonics sound patterns, word families and sight words through the use of poems. Each page targets a different skill and invites your child to write the sound pattern or sight word to complete the poem. Your child will benefit from the explicit instruction and repeated practice.

How to use this book

1. Introduce the target sound pattern or sight word at the top of the page to your child.

2. Let your child complete the poem by writing the target sound pattern or sight word on the lines.

3. Read the completed poem aloud with your child several times to practice his pronunciation and vocabulary.

4. Introduce the interactive activity after the poem and encourage your child to complete it with crayons or colored pencils.

5. Praise and encourage your child at the end of the activity by coloring the stars at the bottom of the page.

6. Reinforce your child's learning with an extension activity from page 80. These activities provide additional practice, and improve fluency and comprehension.

Note: To avoid the awkward 'he or she' construction, the pronouns on this page and page 80 will refer to the male gender.

Contents

Phonics and Word Families

Short Vowel *a* 5
Word Family *at* 6
Word Family *an* 7
Word Family *ad* 8
Word Family *ap* 9
Short Vowel *e* 10
Word Family *ed* 11
Word Family *end* 12
Word Family *ell* 13
Short Vowel *i* 14
Word Family *ip* 15
Word Family *in* 16
Word Family *it* 17
Word Family *ill* 18
Word Family *ick* 19
Short Vowel *o* 20
Word Family *op* 21
Word Family *ot* 22
Short Vowel *u* 23
Word Family *ub* 24
Word Family *ug* 25
Long Vowel *ai* 26
Word Family *ail* 27
Long Vowel *ay* 28
Word Family *ay* 29
Long Vowel *ea* 30
Word Family *eat* 31
Long Vowel *ee* 32
Word Family *eed* 33
Word Family *eep* 34
Long Vowel *oa* 35

Word Family *oat* 36
Consonant Digraph *th* 37
Consonant Digraph *sh* 38
Consonant Digraph *ch* 39
Consonant Digraph *wh* 40

Sight Words

Sight Word *the* 41
Sight Word *to* 42
Sight Word *and* 43
Sight Word *a* 44
Sight Word *I* 45
Sight Word *you* 46
Sight Word *it* 47
Sight Word *in* 48
Sight Word *said* 49
Sight Word *for* 50
Sight Word *up* 51
Sight Word *look* 52
Sight Word *is* 53
Sight Word *go* 54
Sight Word *we* 55
Sight Word *this* 56
Sight Word *little* 57
Sight Word *down* 58
Sight Word *can* 59
Sight Word *see* 60
Sight Word *not* 61
Sight Word *one* 62
Sight Word *me* 63
Sight Word *my* 64
Sight Word *come* 65

Sight Word *with* 66
Sight Word *where* 67
Sight Word *make* 68
Sight Word *find* 69
Sight Word *he* 70
Sight Word *was* 71
Sight Word *that* 72
Sight Word *on* 73
Sight Word *they* 74
Sight Word *all* 75
Sight Word *there* 76
Sight Word *be* 77
Sight Word *have* 78
Sight Word *am* 79

Extension Activities 80

Short Vowel *a*

Date: _____

Write **a** on the lines.

I Can

I c__a__n swing a b___t
in my baseball c__p.
I c__n pet the c__t
sitting on my l__p.
I c__n do all these, —
then I n__p, n__p, n__p!

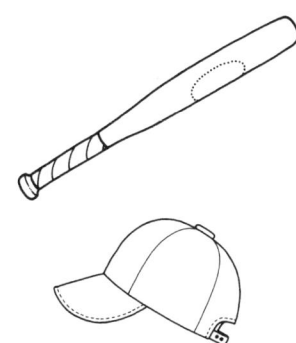

Draw something you **can** do.

To parents: Go to page 80 and do Activity 1 or 4 with your child.

You did a great job!

Word Family at

Date: _____

Write the word family on the lines.

Pat the Bat

Meet P̲a̲t̲ the B____, and her friends, C____ and R____.
But whatever you do, don't step on her m____ ...
P____ the B____ doesn't like th____.

Color **Pat's mat** any way you like.

To parents — Go to page 80 and do Activity 2, 3 or 4 with your child.

Well done! You did great!

6

Word Family an

Date: _____

Write the word family on the lines.

A Plan and a Van

Dan is a m____ with a pl____.

St____ is a m____ with a v____.

What might these two do,

D____ with his pl____

and St____ with his v____?

Draw what you think **Dan** and **Stan** might do with their **plan** and their **van**.

To parents — Go to page 80 and do Activity 2, 3 or 4 with your child.

Amazing job!

Word Family ad

Write the word family on the lines.

Feelings

Br__ad__ felt m____.
T____ felt s____.
They both felt b____,
but Ch____ felt gl____.
M____, s____, b____, gl____ —
these are all feelings that the
friends h____.

Draw a picture of something that might make **Chad** feel **glad**.

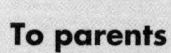
Chad

To parents Go to page 80 and do Activity 2, 3 or 4 with your child.

Fantastic job!

Word Family ap

Date: _____

Write the word family on the lines.

Zap the Firefly

Zap didn't want to n____.

He wanted to fl____

and sn____ and y____.

But soon Z____

was a tired little ch____.

So he turned off his light

and took a n____.

Color **Zap** the Firefly.

| To parents | Go to page 80 and do Activity 2, 3 or 4 with your child. |

Great job!
☆ ☆ ☆

Short Vowel e   Date: _____

Write *e* on the lines.

Hens on the Bed

Ten red hens,
jumping on the bed.
One fell off! The others said,
"Did you hurt your leg?
Should we call the vet?"
But the hen said, "No,
the fun is not over yet!"

Color each **hen red**.
Count them out loud until you get to **ten**.

To parents Go to page 80 and do Activity 1 or 4 with your child.

Brilliant job!

Word Family ed

Date: _____

Write the word family on the lines.

Red, Red, Red

Ned had a r___ b___.

T___ had a r___ sl___.

Fr___ had a r___ sh___.

N___, T___, Fr___.

B___, sl___, sh___.

R___, r___, r___!

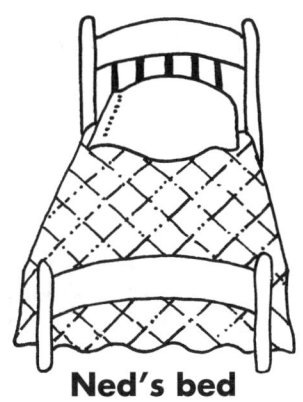
Ned's bed

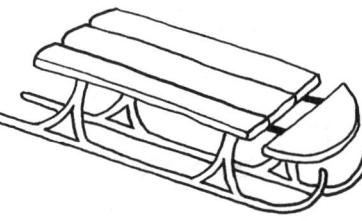
Ted's sled

Fred's shed

Color **Ned's bed**, **Ted's sled** and **Fred's shed**.
Use **red**. Then draw something of yours that is **red**.

| To parents | Go to page 80 and do Activity 2, 3 or 4 with your child. |

Great job!

11

Word Family end Date: _____

Write the word family on the lines.

Spelling Tricks

Read this word: b<u>end</u>

Add an *l*: bl____

Read this word: s____

Add a *p*: sp____

B____, bl____

S____, sp____

Now you're at the very ____!

To whom do you want to **send** a letter in the mail?
Write the person's name on the envelope.

To parents Go to page 80 and do Activity 2, 3 or 4 with your child.

Brilliant job!
☆ ☆ ☆

Word Family

Date: _____

Write the word family on the lines.

Spelling Test

Tell me, t____ me:

Can you sp____ b____?

Can you sp____ f____?

Can you sp____ s____?

Can you sp____ sh____?

Give a great big y____!

You can sp____ very w____!

What else can you do **well**? Draw it here.

To parents Go to page 80 and do Activity 2, 3 or 4 with your child.

Well done! You did great!

Short Vowel i

Write *i* on the lines.

Baby's New Bib

Grandma made a baby bib

with her sewing k__t.

She cut the cloth and used a p__n

to make the new b__b f__t.

Then she sewed the b__b together

b__t by b__t by b__t!

Draw **six** circles on the **bib**. Then color the **bib**.

To parents Go to page 80 and do Activity 1 or 4 with your child.

You did an awesome job!

Word Family ip

Date: _____

Write the word family on the lines.

A Trip to Blip

Take a trip to Planet Bl___.

Zoom around in a spacesh___.

You'll love it there.

You'll really fl___!

What do you think Planet **Blip** looks like?
Color the circle to look like Planet **Blip**.

To parents Go to page 80 and do Activity 2, 3 or 4 with your child.

You did a super job!

Word Family in

Date: _____

Write the word family on the lines.

Chicken Pox!

I have so many all over my skin.

I have got six of them

just on my ch___.

I'm itching so badly,

it makes my head sp___!

Draw something that might make your head **spin**!

To parents Go to page 80 and do Activity 2, 3 or 4 with your child.

Fantastic job!

Word Family it

Date: _____

Write the word family on the lines.

In the City of -it

In the trees, you can see the butterflies fl__it__.

At the diner, you can make a banana spl_____.

On the park benches, you can s_____ and kn_____.

You can do all of these in the City of –it!

What would you like to do in the City of **-it**? Draw **it** in the box.

To parents Go to page 80 and do Activity 2, 3 or 4 with your child.

You did an amazing job!

Word Family

Date: _____

Write the word family on the lines.

The Hill of -ill

What will you do

on the H___ of -ill?

You w___ see Jack,

and you w___ see J___.

You w___ even help

cook on the gr___.

The H___ of -ill

is really a thr___!

Draw yourself sitting at the top of the **hill**.

To parents Go to page 80 and do Activity 2, 3 or 4 with your child.

Great job!

Word Family ick

Date: _____

Write the word family on the lines.

Sick Rick

My dog Rick got s____.

He wouldn't chase his st____

or do his tr____.

Then Dr. N____ pulled

a t____ off R____!

And R____ felt better

very qu____.

Color **Rick**. Write his name on his bowl.

To parents: Go to page 80 and do Activity 2, 3 or 4 with your child.

Amazing job!

Short Vowel o

Write *o* on the lines.

Dot to Dot

In d_o_t to d__t, your j__b is this:
H__p from d__t to d__t.
Draw lines as you go.
Oh, what have you g__t?
A f__x on a b__x, by a l__g.
It's all made of d__ts!

Connect the **dots**. Then color the picture. What is the name of your **fox**? Write it here:
_____

To parents Go to page 80 and do Activity 1 or 4 with your child.

Fantastic job!

Word Family op

Write the word family on the lines.

Date: _____

The Land of -op

There's a place where you
can watch popcorn p__op__,
or h____ on a hill
way up to the t____.
Even when you're ready to dr____,
in the Land of -op,
you just can't st____!

Color the sign.
Then draw a **shop** at the **top** of the hill.

To parents Go to page 80 and do Activity 2, 3 or 4 with your child.

Super job!

Word Family ot

Date: _____

Write the word family on the lines.

Dot's Spots

Dot the Leopard
is proud of each sp___.
They're small and black,
like a domino d___!
Sp___, d___, sp___, d___.
D___ the Leopard
really has quite a l___.

Draw **dots** and **spots** on **Dot** the Leopard.

To parents Go to page 80 and do Activity 2, 3 or 4 with your child.

Fantastic!

Short Vowel u

Date: _____

Write **u** on the lines.

Mom's Tea Party

A c_u_p of tea,
an apple b_u_n.
Toast c_u_t in four,
y_u_m, y_u_m, y_u_m!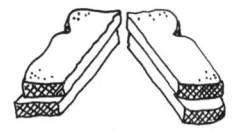
Milk in a m_u_g,
a kiss and a h_u_g.
Mom's tea party
is f_u_n, f_u_n, f_u_n!

Color the **mug**.
What would you like to have in it?

To parents Go to page 80 and do Activity 1 or 4 with your child.

You did a brilliant job!

Word Family ub

Date: _____

Write the word family on the lines.

The Clean Cub Club

R_ub_-a-d____-d____,

Three c____s in a t____.

Scr____, scr____, scr____ —

They're the clean c____ cl____!

Color the **cubs** in the **tub**.

To parents Go to page 80 and do Activity 2, 3 or 4 with your child.

Awesome work!

Word Family ug

Write the word family on the lines.

A Snug Bug

How does a bug

get sn___ in a r___?

First he drinks cocoa

from a nice warm m___.

Then from his dad,

he gets a big h___.

Draw a **bug** on the **rug**.

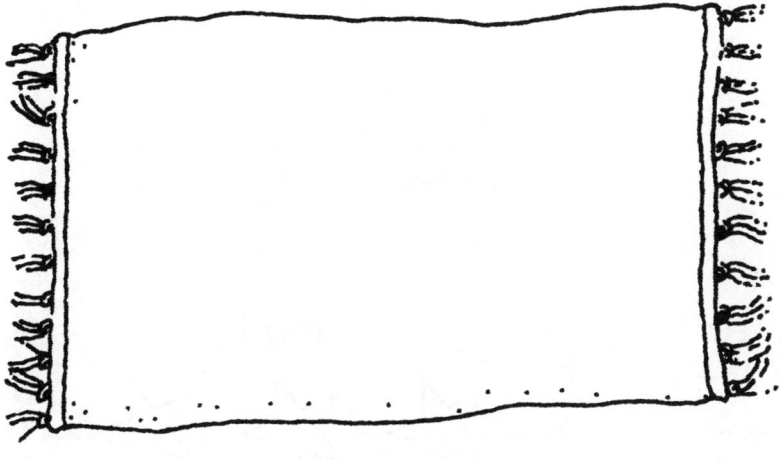

To parents Go to page 80 and do Activity 2, 3 or 4 with your child.

You did an amazing job!

Long Vowel ai

Date: _____

Write **ai** on the lines.

Waiting

W_ai_t for a tr___n to leave.

W___t for r___n to stop.

W___t for p___nt to dry.

W___t for corn to pop.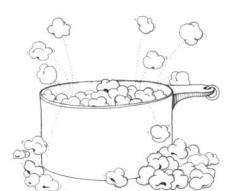

Sometimes it's hard

to w___t, w___t, w___t!

Draw something you have to **wait** for.

To parents — Go to page 80 and do Activity 1 or 4 with your child.

Neat!

Word Family ail

Date: _____

Write the word family on the lines.

Two Snails

One sn**ail** goes to get the m____.

Another sn____ picks

flowers to put in a p____.

Each sn____ stops

to watch a boat lift its s____.

Then each sn____ moves

along its own little tr____.

Color each **snail** purple.
Color each **trail** green.

To parents Go to page 80 and do Activity 2, 3 or 4 with your child.

Super job at reading!

Long Vowel

Date: _____

Write **ay** on the lines.

Spring Play Day

A good w*ay* to spend a d___ is to fill it with lots of pl___. Sail a boat on the b___, l___ down in a pile of h___, and invite a blue j___ to come and st___!

Draw a game or sport you like to **play**.

To parents — Go to page 80 and do Activity 1 or 4 with your child.

Well done! You did great!

28

Word Family _ay_

Date: _____

Write the word family on the lines.

Go Away, Rain!

Rain, rain, go aw___.
The children s___
they want to pl___.
Sun, Sun, come and st___.
The children s___
they're tired of gr___!

Draw what you might do on a rainy **day** and on a sunny **day**.

To parents — Go to page 80 and do Activity 2, 3 or 4 with your child.

You did an amazing job!

29

Long Vowel ea

Write **ea** on the lines.

A Feast

A big m__ea__l is a tr__ea__t.

__Ea__t some b__ea__ns and m__ea__t.

Drink a s__ea__ of t__ea__.

__Ea__t some bread — whole wh__ea__t.

Then have a h__ea__p of p__ea__s.

And last, p__ea__ches and cr__ea__m.

Now your plate is cl__ea__n!

What food would be at your **feast**? Draw it here.

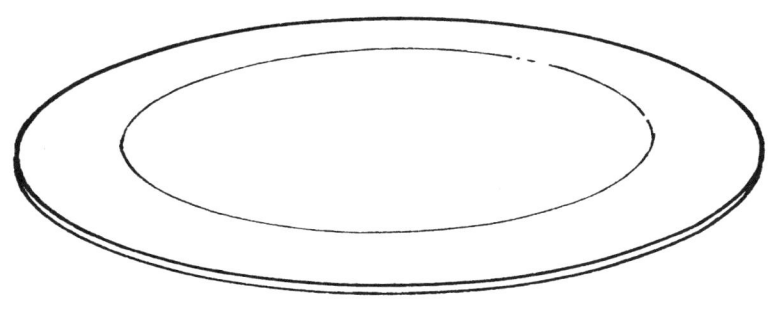

To parents Go to page 80 and do Activity 1 or 4 with your child.

Well done!

Word Family _eat

Date: _____

Write the word family on the lines.

Beat the Heat

How can you b~~eat~~

summer h____, h____, h____?

Have an ice cream

for a tr____, tr____, tr____.

Then jump in the pool —

N____, n____, n____!

Draw something you do to **beat** the **heat**.

To parents Go to page 80 and do Activity 2, 3 or 4 with your child.

Super job at reading!

Long Vowel ee

Write **ee** on the lines.

Date: _____

Driving a Jeep

We're steering in our j__ee__p,

hearing horns go b____p,

down a hill so st____p.

We always check our sp____d —

now gas is all we n____d!

Color the **jeep**.

beep
beep
beep

To parents Go to page 80 and do Activity 1 or 4 with your child.

You did an awesome job!

Word Family eed

Write the word family on the lines.

Plant a Seed

Plant a seed. Pull a w_____.
What else does a garden n_____?
Soil, sun, water and time.
A gardener works hard —
there are people to f_____.

Draw vegetables in the garden.
Draw some **weeds**, too!

To parents Go to page 80 and do Activity 2, 3 or 4 with your child.

You did great!

Word Family eep

Date: _____

Write the word family on the lines.

Counting Sheep

If you really cannot sl___,
then try to count sh___.
Keep counting sh___
until you fall asl___.
But do not count baby birds —
they will keep you awake,
because they p___
and ch___ and ch___!

Color the **sheep**. Then count them.

To parents — Go to page 80 and do Activity 2, 3 or 4 with your child.

Brilliant!

Long Vowel  Date: _____

Write **oa** on the lines.

Winter Breakfast

Cereal fl__oa__ts in milk.

____ts are in my bowl.

T____st is on my plate.

Potatoes r____st on the stove.

The dishes s____k.

I put on my c____t.

I'm ready for the cold!

What else would you like on your breakfast plate? Draw it.

To parents Go to page 80 and do Activity 1 or 4 with your child.

Well done! You did great!

Word Family oat

Date: _____

Write the word family on the lines.

Row Your Boat

Row, row, row your b<u>oat</u>

gently in the lake.

Don't forget to wear

your c_____.

It's cold, for goodness' sake!

Draw yourself in the **boat**.
Don't forget your **coat**!

To parents Go to page 80 and do Activity 2, 3 or 4 with your child.

Amazing job!

Consonant Digraph th

Date: _____

Write **th** on the lines.

This and That

__This and __at,

__ese and __ose.

And __at thing

over __ere.

__ese are words

__at you will pull out

to show what

you are talking about!

Trace the **th-** words.
Then read them aloud.

To parents Go to page 80 and do Activity 1 or 4 with your child.

Well done!

Consonant Digraph sh

Write **sh** on the lines.

Sherry Shepard

Sh___erry ___epard could not sleep.

So ___e tried

to count some ___eep.

BAA! Those ___eep made such a

fuss that ___erry ___epard

___outed "___USH!"

SHUSH!

Color **Sherry Shepard** and the **sheep**. Then tell them, "**Shush!**"

To parents — Go to page 80 and do Activity 1 or 4 with your child.

Great job!

38

Consonant Digraph ch

Date: _____

Write **ch** on the lines.

Charlie's Cafe

__Ch__ildren, pull up a __ch__air.

From this menu you can __ch__oose.

Potato __ch__ips or __ch__opped fruit.

A __ch__eeseburger or __ch__icken soup.

__Ch__ocolate __ch__ip cookies

or __ch__erry pie.

__Ch__ew your food,

get the __ch__eck,

then say goodbye!

What **ch-** food will you **choose**? Circle it.

To parents — Go to page 80 and do Activity 1 or 4 with your child.

You did great!

39

Consonant Digraph wh

Write **wh** on the lines.

Question Words

Who and ~~wh~~at?
___en and ___ere?
___y and how?
All these words
are ones you will use,
___en you want
an answer NOW!

What, **when**, **where** and **why** are all question words. Color the question marks in different colors.

To parents Go to page 80 and do Activity 1 or 4 with your child.

Great work!

Sight Word the

Date: _____

Write the sight word on the lines.

In My Book

I see ~~the~~ apple.

I see _____ ant.

I see _____ little bug

on _____ green plant.

I see _____ spider

in my book.

I see _____ turtle.

Have a look!

Find **the** apple, little bug and turtle. Then color them.

To parents Go to page 80 and do Activity 1, 2, 3 or 5 with your child.

Great work!

Sight Word to

Date: _____

Write the sight word on the lines.

I Like School

I like ___to___ read.

I like _____ write.

I like _____ share

and _____ be polite.

I like _____ paint.

I like _____ count.

I like school, that's right!

Draw something that you like about school.

To parents Go to page 80 and do Activity 1, 2, 3 or 5 with your child.

You did a brilliant job!

42

Sight Word

Date: _____

Write the sight word on the lines.

My Pet

My pet can run,
and jump _____ bark.
My pet can walk
to the store _____ the park.
My pet can eat,
_____ sleep _____ play.
I hug my pet every day!

Color the dog **and** give him a name.

_____

To parents — Go to page 80 and do Activity 1, 2, 3 or 5 with your child.

You did great!
☆ ☆ ☆

Sight Word a

Write the sight word on the lines.

Colors

Orange is a carrot.

Yellow is ___ pear.

Green is the grass.

Brown is ___ bear.

Purple is ___ plum.

Blue is the sky.

Black is ___ funny hat.

Red is ___ cherry pie!

Color the color wheel. Trace the letter **a** in the wheel.

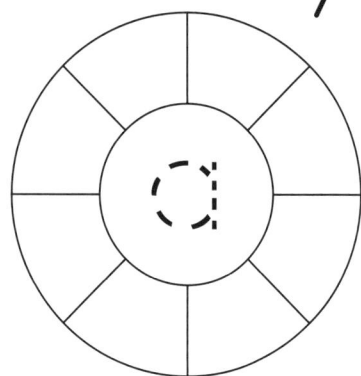

To parents Go to page 80 and do Activity 1, 2, 3 or 5 with your child.

Well done! You did great!

Sight Word I

Date: _____

Write the sight word on the lines.

I Can!

I can jump.

__ can run.

__ can play in the sun.

__ can swim.

__ can skate.

__ can bake a cake!

Draw yourself doing your favorite activity.
Finish the sentence.

To parents Go to page 80 and do Activity 1, 2, 3 or 5 with your child.

"I can _____!"

Fantastic work!

Sight Word: you

Write the sight word on the lines.

Can You See a Rainbow?

Can <u>you</u> see red?

Can _____ see orange?

Can _____ see yellow,

green, blue and purple?

Can _____ see colors

way up high?

Can _____ see a rainbow

in the sky?

How many colors of the rainbow can **you** find in your room?

To parents: Go to page 80 and do Activity 1, 2, 3 or 5 with your child.

Amazing work!

Sight Word

Date: _____

Write the sight word on the lines.

What Is It?

Is ___it___ red?

Is ___ black, with spots on its back?

Is ___ small?

Is ___ round?

Can ___ fly all around?

Is ___ a ladybug I just found?

Draw a ladybug on the hand.

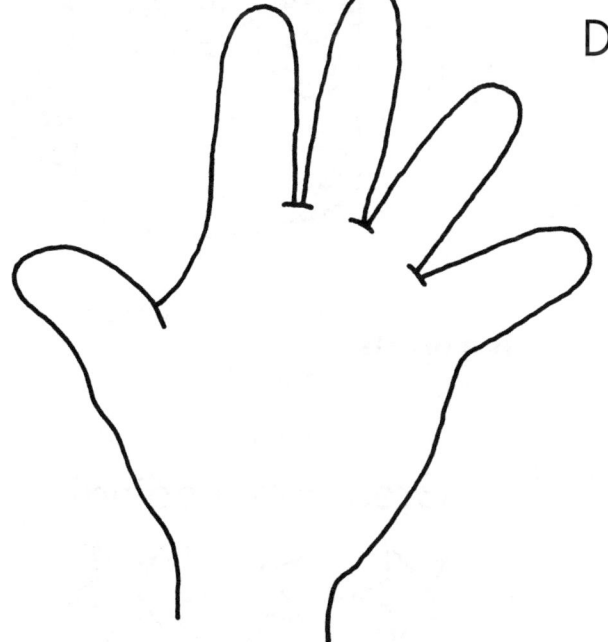

To parents Go to page 80 and do Activity 1, 2, 3 or 5 with your child.

Super job at reading!
☆ ☆ ☆

Sight Word in

Write the sight word on the lines.

Mix the Soup!

Mix in   the potatoes.

Mix ___ the peas.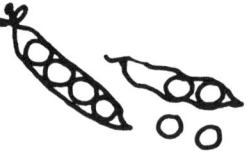

Mix ___ the tomatoes,

if you please.

Mix ___ the corn.

Mix ___ the carrots.

M–m–m–m! Yummy soup!

Draw something else you would like to add to your soup.

To parents Go to page 80 and do Activity 1, 2, 3 or 5 with your child.

Great job reading!

Sight Word said

Date: _____

Write the sight word on the lines.

Animal Talk

"Bow-wow," said the dog.

"Meow," _____ the cat.

"Quack, quack," _____ the duck.

"Who, who," _____ the owl.

"Chirp, chirp," _____ the bird.

"Moo, moo," _____ the cow.

"QUIET!" _____ the sleepy farmer.

Write what the farmer said to the animals.

To parents Go to page 80 and do Activity 1, 2, 3 or 5 with your child.

Neat work!

Sight Word for

Date: _____

Write the sight word on the lines.

What Goes Together?

An apple <u>for</u> a teacher,

a bone _____ a dog,

a nut _____ a squirrel,

a fly _____ a frog,

a mat _____ a cat,

a flower _____ a bee,

a worm _____ a bird,

a friend _____ me!

Tell your friend what you would like to get **for** your birthday.

To parents Go to page 80 and do Activity 1, 2, 3 or 5 with your child.

Fantastic job!

Sight Word  up

Date: _____

Write the sight word on the lines.

The Rooster

He wakes  the cow.

He wakes _____ the dog.

He wakes _____ all the sheep.

He wakes _____ the ducks.

He wakes _____ the farmer,

and then goes back to sleep!

Write the name of the person who wakes you **up** each morning.

_____
_____

To parents Go to page 80 and do Activity 1, 2, 3 or 5 with your child.

You did a brilliant job!

51

Sight Word look

Date: _____

Write the sight word on the lines.

Silly Rhymes

Oh, ~~look~~, _____ at the bug.

It is on the rug.

Oh, _____, _____ at the fly.

It is on the pie.

Oh, _____, _____ at the bee.

It is in the tree!

Now try your own!

Oh, look, look at the _____.

It is on the _____.

To parents — Go to page 80 and do Activity 1, 2, 3 or 5 with your child.

Brilliant job! Well done!
☆ ☆ ☆

Sight Word is

Date: _____

Write the sight word on the lines.

What Color?

An apple ‾is‾ red.

A blueberry ____ blue.

A banana ____ yellow.

A lemon ____, too.

A carrot ____ orange.

An orange ____, too.

Fruits and vegetables are good for you!

What is your favorite fruit or vegetable?
_____
_____

To parents Go to page 80 and do Activity 1, 2, 3 or 5 with your child.

Great job!

Sight Word go

Write the sight word on the lines.

Date: _____

I Go

I _go_ in a bus.
I ____ in a car.
I ____ someplace near.
I ____ someplace far.
I ____ on a bike.
I ____ for a cone.
I ____, ____, ____.
Then I ____ home.

Where do you **go** on a Sunday?
_____
_____

To parents Go to page 80 and do Activity 1, 2, 3 or 5 with your child.

Amazing!
☆ ☆ ☆

Sight Word we   Date: _____

Write the sight word on the lines.

What Do Kids Like?

Do kids like to skate?

Yes, we do!

Do kids like to play?

Yes, ____ do!

Do kids like to swim
on a sunny day?

Yes, ____ do!

Do kids like soccer?

Yes, yes, yes!

Yes, ____ do!

To parents Go to page 80 and do Activity 1, 2, 3 or 5 with your child.

Brilliant!
☆ ☆ ☆

Which of these activities do you enjoy the most? Color the picture.

55

Sight Word this

Date: _____

Write the sight word on the lines.

I See This

I see ~~this~~ frog.

I see _____ cat.

I see _____ bird.

I see _____ rat.

I see _____ mouse.

It is small.

I see _____ dog

who chases them all!

Write the name of your favorite animal.

_____

To parents Go to page 80 and do Activity 1, 2, 3 or 5 with your child.

Great job reading!

Sight Word little

Date: _____

Write the sight word on the lines.

One Little Blue Bird

One ~~little~~ blue bird

sitting in a tree.

Two _____ yellow fish

swimming in the sea.

Three _____ orange crabs

crawling in the sand.

Four _____ brown worms

crawling in my hand!

Count the fingers on one hand.

To parents Go to page 80 and do Activity 1, 2, 3 or 5 with your child.

Super job at spelling!

Sight Word down

Date: _____

Write the sight word on the lines.

Autumn Leaves

Red leaves fall down.

Green leaves fall _____.

Orange leaves fall _____,

all over the town.

Yellow leaves fall _____.

Brown leaves fall _____.

Autumn leaves fall _____,

and cover the ground.

Color each leaf in a different color: red, green, orange, yellow and brown.

To parents Go to page 80 and do Activity 1, 2, 3 or 5 with your child.

Fantastic job at spelling!

Sight Word can

Date: _____

Write the sight word on the lines.

I Can Hop

I can hop like a frog.
I ____ swim like a fish.
I ____ look at a star.
I ____ make a wish!
I ____ hop like a bunny.
I ____ creep and leap.
I ____ go to bed.
I ____ fall asleep.

Good Night!

Count the stars on this page.

To parents Go to page 80 and do Activity 1, 2, 3 or 5 with your child.

You can spell very well!

Sight Word see

Date: _____

Write the sight word on the lines.

I See

I ~~see~~ a cat.

I _____ a dog.

I _____ a turtle.

I _____ a frog.

I _____ a ladybug.

I _____ a bee.

I _____ a spider.

A spider sees me!

Draw a spider in the web.

To parents — Go to page 80 and do Activity 1, 2, 3 or 5 with your child.

You can spell very well!
☆ ☆ ☆

60

Sight Word not

Date: _____

Write the sight word on the lines.

What Am I?

I am ~~not~~ a cat.

I am _____ a dog.

I am _____ a spider.

I am _____ a frog.

I am _____ a fish.

I am _____ a slug.

What am I?

I am a bug!

Color the bug.

To parents Go to page 80 and do Activity 1, 2, 3 or 5 with your child.

Great job at spelling!

Sight Word one

Date: _____

Write the sight word on the lines.

One Yummy Lunch

I have ~~one~~ sandwich.

I have _____ drink, too.

I have two cookies.

I will give _____ to you.

I have some grapes.

I have _____ bunch.

I have _____ big and yummy lunch!

Draw your favorite lunch food.

To parents — Go to page 80 and do Activity 1, 2, 3 or 5 with your child.

You can spell very well!

62

Sight Word me

Date: _____

Write the sight word on the lines.

Can You See Me?

Can you see ~~me~~?

That is ____ near the tree.

Can you see ____?

That is ____ under the tree.

Can you see ____?

That is ____ in the tree.

Come up in the tree
and be with ____!

Trace the words. Color the tree.

~~This is me~~.

To parents Go to page 80 and do Activity 1, 2, 3 or 5 with your child.

You can spell very well!

Sight Word my

Write the sight word on the lines.

Date: _____

Good Helper

I can feed _my_ pet.

I can make ____ bed.

I can put away ____ books,

after they have been read.

I can do ____ jobs

that I have to do.

I can be a good helper,

just like you!

Trace the word '**broom**'.
Color the broom.

To parents — Go to page 80 and do Activity 1, 2, 3 or 5 with your child.

Fantastic job at spelling!
☆ ☆ ☆

Sight Word come

Date: _____

Write the sight word on the lines.

Please Come See

Please ~~come~~ see my cat.

Please _____ see my dog.

Please _____ see my fish.

Please _____ see my frog.

Please _____ see my bird, too.

Please _____ see my pets.

Please take one home with you!

Draw a pet you would like to have.

To parents Go to page 80 and do Activity 1, 2, 3 or 5 with your child.

You are a great speller!

Sight Word with

Date: _____

Write the sight word on the lines.

With You

I will run _with_ you.

I will play _____ you.

I will read _____ you,

and ride bikes _____ you.

I will be _____ you

to the very end.

All because I am a friend!

Draw a picture of your best friend.

To parents Go to page 80 and do Activity 1, 2, 3 or 5 with your child.

You are a brilliant speller!

Sight Word

Date: _____

Write the sight word on the lines.

Where, Oh Where?

Oh ~~where~~, oh _____

has my little dog gone?

Oh _____, oh _____

can he be?

His tail is short.

And his ears are long.

Oh _____, oh _____ is he?

Color the girl and her dog.

To parents Go to page 80 and do Activity 1, 2, 3 or 5 with your child.

You can spell very well!

Sight Word make   Date: _____

Write the sight word on the lines.

Ten Little Dogs

I have ten little dogs,

and they belong to me.

I can _make_ them do tricks.

Do you want to see?

I can _____ them jump high,

and _____ them jump low.

I can _____ them roll over,

and sit just so.

Name any two tricks that you would want to teach the dogs.

To parents Go to page 80 and do Activity 1, 2, 3 or 5 with your child.

Great job spelling!

Sight Word

Date: _____

Write the sight word on the lines.

What Can You Find?

Can you ~~find~~ the eggs?
Can you _____ all ten?
Can you _____ the mother hen?
Can you _____ the bees?
Can you _____ all five?
Can you _____ the bees in the hive?

Count the eggs and bees.
Write your answers in the boxes.

To parents Go to page 80 and do Activity 1, 2, 3 or 5 with your child.

You are an amazing speller!

69

Sight Word he

Date: _____

Write the sight word on the lines.

My Turtle

This is my turtle,

and ~~he~~ lives in a shell.

And ____ likes his home very well.

See, ____ pokes his head out

when ____ wants to eat.

And ____ pulls it back in

when ____ wants to sleep!

Color the turtle shell with bright colours.

To parents Go to page 80 and do Activity 1, 2, 3 or 5 with your child.

You are an amazing speller!

Sight Word was

Date: _____

Write the sight word on the lines.

Fuzzy Wuzzy

Fuzzy Wuzzy ~~was~~ a bear.

Fuzzy Wuzzy had no hair.

Fuzzy Wuzzy _____ not fuzzy, _____ he?

No, he _____ not!

Write the name of another animal that has fuzzy hair.

_____

To parents Go to page 80 and do Activity 1, 2, 3 or 5 with your child.

You can spell very well!
☆ ☆ ☆

71

Sight Word that

Date: _____

Write the sight word on the lines.

This and That

This is a mouse,
but ~~that~~ is a rat.

This is a kitten,
but _____ is a cat.

This is a puppy,
but _____ is a dog.

This is a toad,
but _____ is a frog.

Color the smaller animal in each pair of animals.

To parents Go to page 80 and do Activity 1, 2, 3 or 5 with your child.

You are an amazing speller!
☆ ☆ ☆

Sight Word on

Date: _____

Write the sight word on the lines.

Rain

Rain __on__ the green grass.

Rain ____ the tree.

Rain ____ the housetops,

but not ____ me!

Rain ____ the forest.

Rain ____ the sea.

Rain ____ the mountains,

but not ____ me!

Draw yourself under the umbrella.

To parents Go to page 80 and do Activity 1, 2, 3 or 5 with your child.

Great job at spelling!

Sight Word they

Write the sight word on the lines.

Friends

I like friends. Ask me why.

Because 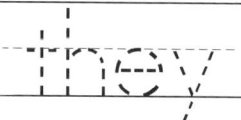 help me.

Because _____ share with me.

Because _____ play with me.

Because _____ tell me jokes.

That is why I like friends!

Write down the games you play with your friends.

To parents Go to page 80 and do Activity 1, 2, 3 or 5 with your child.

Brilliant!

Sight Word

Date: _____

Write the sight word on the lines.

All About Spiders

Do _____ spiders have 8 legs?

Do they _____ have 2 body parts?

Do they _____ hatch from eggs?

Yes, _____ spiders have 8 legs.

Yes, they _____ have 2 body parts.

Yes, they _____ hatch from eggs.

Color the spiders.

To parents — Go to page 80 and do Activity 1, 2, 3 or 5 with your child.

Super job!

Sight Word there

Date: _____

Write the sight word on the lines.

Over There

Over ~~there~~ on the ground,
over _____ on the grass,
over _____ on the tree,
is something to see.

Over _____ on the ground,
over _____ on the grass,
over _____ on the tree,
is little me!

Color the boy on the tree.

To parents Go to page 80 and do Activity 1, 2, 3 or 5 with your child.

Well done!

Sight Word be

Date: _____

Write the sight word on the lines.

I Can Be Anything

I can ~~be~~ a doctor.

I can ____ a teacher.

I can ____ a clown.

I can ____ a creature.

I can ____ a spider.

I can ____ a bee.

I can ____ anything

I want to ____!

Write down what you want to be when you grow up.

_____
_____
_____

To parents Go to page 80 and do Activity 1, 2, 3 or 5 with your child.

Fantastic job!
☆ ☆ ☆

Sight Word have

Date: _____

Write the sight word on the lines.

I Have

I have two eyes.
I _____ one nose.
I _____ ten fingers.
I _____ ten toes.
I _____ two ears.
I _____ two feet, too.
I _____ one big smile
. . . just for you!

Draw yourself.

To parents Go to page 80 and do Activity 1, 2, 3 or 5 with your child.

You are an amazing speller!

Sight Word

Date: _____

Write the sight word on the lines.

I Am

I am   a spider.

I ____ a fly.

I ____ a pretty butterfly.

I ____ a cat.

I ____ a dog.

I ____ a big, green, jumping frog!

To parents Go to page 80 and do Activity 1, 2, 3 or 5 with your child.

Trace the 'hops' and color the frog.

Great job!

79

Extension Activities

Activity 1: Touchy Letters
Skill: Provides additional practice with target sound pattern or sight word
Fill a shallow container with sand for your child to use for letter tracing. For instance, on the day your child is working on the *oo* sound, let him use his fingers to trace the letters *oo* into the sand as you read aloud *broom*, *food*, *mood* and so on. Depending on your child's ability, he might write the entire word as you dictate. (As an alternative to using sand, you may complete this activity with paper and crayons.)

Activity 2: Mystery Word
Skill: Provides additional practice with target word family or sight word
After your child is very familiar with a poem, have him close his book so he cannot see it. Read the poem aloud, pausing when you come to the target word. Challenge your child to call out the word that belongs there. If your child needs help, you can give him the first letter in the word.

Activity 3: Password Fun
Skill: Provides additional practice with target word family or sight word
Write the target word(s) on index cards or sticky notes and paste each of them on a doorframe in the house. Have your child read the 'password' every time he passes through the door.

Activity 4: Read, Read, Read
Skill: Builds fluency
Read the poem several times aloud, tracking the print with your finger and inviting your child to join you as much as he is able. Then invite your child to read the poem in different voices: softly, loudly, quickly, slowly, baby voice, deep voice, squeaky voice and so on. Your child can also mime the actions in the poem as he reads.

Activity 5: Poem Scramble
Skill: Builds comprehension — story sequence
Copy the poem onto a sheet of paper and cut the lines of the poem apart into strips. Challenge your child to put the strips back into the order of the poem. For additional challenge, cut apart the words of the poem and have him put the words in order to recreate the poem.